GW00870924

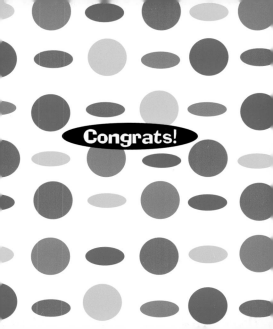

Congrats!

A Tale
of
Success

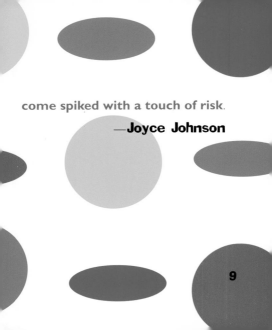

come spiked with a touch of risk.

—Joyce Johnson

9

Some of life's sweetest moments

Congrats!

Congratulations! Whether you've just accomplished something you worked hard for or you're on the road to **success** at whatever you've chosen to dedicate yourself to, this book is meant to inspire **you.** **Believing** in yourself, knowing the true meaning of success, and aspiring to the heights reached by others will get **you** where you **want** to be—in all facets of your life.

Introduction

Congrats!

Congrats!

ISBN: 0-7407-3874-7

Library of Congress Catalog Card Number: 2003102680

Congrats!

Edited by Tracy Guth Spangler

Designed by Diane Hobbing

Ariel Books

Andrews McMeel Publishing

Kansas City

My parents taught me that the only failure is not to have tried. To try and have *any* result is a success: Either it works out as you thought it would, better than you thought, or differently than you thought. Moving to New York City is a pretty big accomplishment for me—I had to try it, to test my abilities as a dancer next to the best in the field. I've learned to survive in the city, and I've learned and grown as an artist.

—Lisa, New York, New York

You *did* it! Remember when this was just the inkling of a dream, a doodle on a pad of paper, a glimmer of hope in the back of your mind? Luxuriate in the knowledge that you made it happen!

Congrats!

I am

no longer what I was.

I will **remain** what I

have become.

—Coco Chanel

13

Even

with the **best** of maps

and instruments, we can never

fully chart our journeys.

—**Gail Pool**

Congrats!

One vital ingredient of success: patience. Great ideas and plans need to incubate. Give yourself the space and time to prepare, nurture, and harvest, and don't allow yourself to wallow if things don't always go your way. Everything *doesn't* have to happen right now.

15

The best way to predict

Congrats!

your future is to create it.
—Patti LaBelle

17

Okay, maybe not everyone is happy for you—people are caught up in their own ambitions, frustrations, and disappointments. Share your success with a chosen few whom you know will be truly, selflessly thrilled. Don't boast or use your success as revenge; just be happy in it for yourself, not for how it makes you look compared to others.

There is an **applause** superior to that of the multitudes: one's own.

—Elizabeth Elton Smith

A
Tale
of
Success

My proudest moment was childbirth. After several miscarriages I wondered if I'd ever become a mother. When Sam drew his first breath, I thought, I did it! I had successfully nurtured, grown, and delivered a baby. I felt so triumphant. I was very proud of my body that day.

—Donna, Livingston, New Jersey

There is no point at which you can say, "Well, I'm **successful** now. I might as well take a nap."

—**Carrie Fisher**

Congrats!

Say no to what saps your energy and emotion so you can say yes to what's important. You can't succeed at what matters if you're preoccupied with what doesn't.

it's possible.

—Marion Jones

25

A
Tale
of
Success

s it too cheesy to tell you that my greatest accomplishment is to keep my understanding and lovely wife by my side so that we could have and raise two beautiful, crazy, energetic little girls and share them with the world?

—Trent, Nashville, Tennessee

On the road to success, there are times when you feel you're going anywhere but in the right direction. It's okay. Give yourself a time-out, and take care of yourself. Things will pick up tomorrow or next week or next month.

Congrats!

The trouble with fulfilling your **ambitions** is you think you will be transformed into some sort of archangel and you're not. You still have to wash your socks.

—**Louis de Bernières**

To **follow** without halt,

one aim; there is the secret of success.

And success? What is it? I do not find it in

the applause of the theater; it lies rather

in the satisfaction of accomplishment.

—Anna Pavlova

Congrats!

Don't mistake perfection for success. Doing something right doesn't necessarily mean doing it perfectly. In fact, spending your time trying to be perfect might mean you never get around to doing what you actually wanted to do in the first place.

vant to be more successful
Connect with friends and colleagues
Meet regularly with a group of
riends—or face-to-face with just
one—and talk about issues in your
ives, what's standing in the way of
goals, and how you can achieve what
you want. You won't believe how
empowering it is.

If you **hear** a voice

within you say "you cannot paint,"

then by all means paint, and that

voice will be silenced.

—Vincent van Gogh

I've grown **tired** of wanting the unattainable. . . . I'm taking a moment of pause to **celebrate** what I already have.

—Isabella Rossellini

Congrats!

Don't feel guilty about your good fortune! You've worked hard for this.

Follow your **dreams** as long as you live!
Never be afraid to go out on the limb to live
up to your **expectations.** Always do
things your way and have **fun!**

—Picabo Street

Congrats!

Keep away from people who try to
belittle your **ambitions.** Small people
always do that, but the really great make you
feel that you, too, can **become great.**

—Mark Twain

37

To really "get ahead," work from your strengths, and don't dwell on your weaknesses.

Congrats!

If you surrender to
the wind, you can **ride** it.
—Toni Morrison

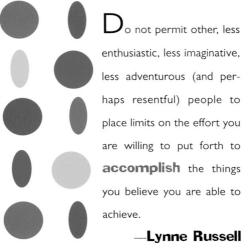

Do not permit other, less enthusiastic, less imaginative, less adventurous (and perhaps resentful) people to place limits on the effort you are willing to put forth to **accomplish** the things you believe you are able to achieve.

—Lynne Russell

Congrats!

Hope **begins** in the dark, the stubborn hope that if you just show up and try to do the right thing, the dawn will come.

—Anne Lamott

If you're afraid to do something, take that as an indication that you should go for it. Jump off the high board—be confident that you'll break the surface and be able to swim strongly to the side.

Congrats!

One hundred percent of the shots you don't take don't go in.

—Wayne Gretzky

A
Tale
of
Success

I lowered my cholesterol by fifty-eight points through diet and exercise, and no medication! I guess I'm pretty proud of that accomplishment.

—Ron, Arlington Heights, Illinois

45

Whatever it is you do, do it **well** and do it with joy. The best is yet to come.

—Ivana Trump

Congrats!

W e are made to **persist.** That's how we find out who we are.

—Tobias Wolff

Never look to the ground for your next step. Greatness belongs to those who look to the horizon.

—Bud Greenspan

Congrats!

If I died tomorrow, I would have no regrets. If I want to try this or I want to learn that or read this book, I do. I'm curious, I ask questions. I really feel like it's never too late to learn. Everyone has an end, and you may as well live your life now.

—Lucy Liu

49

Dream. **Dream wild.** Extremely wild dreams. Somewhere back there is a wild seed waiting. Of that I am sure.

—Patch Adams

Congrats!

Other people may not have had high **expectations** for me . . . but I had high expectations for myself.

—Shannon Miller

A
Tale
of
Success

In my mid-thirties I moved to Florence, Italy, intending to stay for one year. I fell into the company of painters and musicians and began to write poetry. Four years later, when I returned to the States, I enrolled in an MFA program and began teaching poetry to children. Living abroad completely changed my life. Everyone should do it.

—Mary, Queens, New York

Arriving at

one **goal** is the starting

point to another.

—John Dewey

Congrats!

Pride is often portrayed as a negative, arrogant emotion, but allow yourself to revel in your accomplishment and gain strength, self-trust, and joy from it.

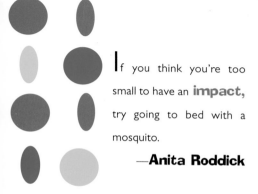

If you think you're too small to have an **impact**, try going to bed with a mosquito.

—Anita Roddick

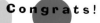

Congrats!

Achievement is not about what you've *done*, but what you've **gained** from your experience.

—Lynn Hill

57

A Tale
of
Success

I am most proud of having put myself through one of the best universities in the country, debt free, with no loans or parental or governmental assistance.

—Raymond, San Diego, California

It's not that I'm so **smart**, it's just that I stay with problems longer. —**Albert Einstein**

Congrats!

True success is something you feel in your bones. It's not just your accomplishment on paper or the way others perceive it. It's being newly centered, suddenly strong.

When there is no road,

Congrats!

you make a road.

—Jenny Lumet

Success often comes with the responsibility of helping others to find success as well.

Congrats!

Life is big, broad, **splendid** in **opportunity.** It is to be used, not cherished. It is to be **spent,** not saved.

—Alice Foote MacDougall

A Tale
of
Success

One of my proudest moments was when I bought my house at age twenty-eight. The first night, I wandered from room to room and could not believe this was mine! Also, I did it on my own. Somehow that makes me more proud.

—**Wendy, Toms River, New Jersey**

Success doesn't come to you. You **go** to it.

—Marva Collins

Congrats!

Life is a verb, **not** a noun.

—**Charlotte Perkins Gilman**

A Tale
of
Success

The moments I am most proud of are when my culinary students mention how great they think my classes are and how they have really learned something. Knowing that they are better cooks because of me is a great feeling.

—Dave, Elkhart, Indiana

Ultimately, you have nothing

Congrats!

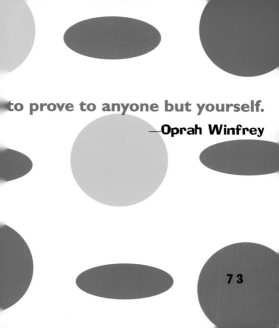

to prove to anyone but yourself.

—Oprah Winfrey

We can do anything we want to do if we stick to it long enough.

—Helen Keller

Congrats!

When you do something you are proud of,
dwell on it a little, **praise** yourself for it.

—Mildred Newman

A Tale
of
Success

I was so proud when I found out I got into MIT's Leaders for Manufacturing program. I earned a Master's in engineering and an MBA simultaneously. I still think back and can't believe I got into MIT! I know it sounds geeky, but for engineers it is a great honor.

**—Jacqueline, San Antonio,
Texas**

Do what you love!

Congrats!

Do it with passion!

—Iyanla Vanzant

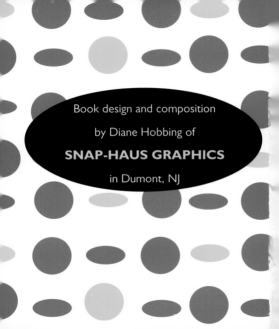

Book design and composition

by Diane Hobbing of

SNAP-HAUS GRAPHICS

in Dumont, NJ